IT'S HARD BUT I'LL LET GO:

Letting Go of someone you really love and break up recovery.

Kristy coble

Table of contents

Chapter 1

MEETING HIM/HER AT THE WRONG TIME

Are You With The Right Person At The Wrong Time? Meeting the perfect person at the wrong moment may seem agonizing

The notion of "right person, wrong time" refers to a relationship with someone who looks ideal for you, but mitigating circumstances are keeping you apart, leaving the potential unmet. Despite the apparent spark, extrinsic elements are dragging the situation down with a feeling of impossibility that may be tough to overcome.

Sometimes individuals who are amazing companions for you, are also folx who are not moving in the same direction in life," For example, one or both persons may be going through something tough, facing a huge life shift, or just aren't presently interested in a relationship.

Since you aren't able to see the relationship through, a "right person, wrong time" scenario may leave you with a worry that you're somehow missing out on this fabled soulmate connection—and make it easy to project dreams onto them.

"You may feel like you have to do everything it takes to make the relationship succeed, even at your disadvantage, since it's the 'right person,'"

When you're presented with the potential of love, you want to think that you would submit totally to the experience—but sometimes life occurs. It's awful when it doesn't work out, but the fact is that the sparkly, thrilling sensations of liking someone come rather regularly in dating.

The actual magic is two individuals deciding to commit to something together.

When you're with the right person at the wrong moment.

Your aims don't meet up.
You have fun together, yet there's a nagging sensation you're on different pages. Maybe their objective is to travel and explore while you're ready to purchase a home and establish a family. To be together, one of you would have to forsake your separate aspirations, which could be too high of a penalty to pay.

If you feel like your objectives are incompatible or would create a lot of hurdles to being together, this might be a clue that it's the wrong time.

When two individuals are headed on the same path in life, there may still be obstacles, but maybe there isn't as much of a hindrance.

One of you is going through something hard. If you're going through a bad period, it might be hard for you to care for yourself, much less offer a relationship the full energy and attention it requires. King writes if this is occurring in the growing connection, it's normal for the relationship to take a backseat as priorities shift toward doing whatever you need to feel better. Unfortunately, keeping a relationship may not be high on your agenda.

There's no reciprocal effort being put into the interaction.

It's crucial that good partnerships have a reciprocal give and take, and it's not one-sided. If you're finding yourself too busy to text back or follow up on dates, use it as a clue that you aren't able to devote the emotional energy and/or time that's necessary for a growing relationship. Relationships take work If it seems like you both continually running into situations where one (or both) of you can't give enough energy to the relationship, that might be an indication it's the wrong time.

There are a lot of life changes occurring.
For the most part, relationships require a certain degree of consistency to establish something permanent and steady. if there are too many shifting parts—for example, family concerns, significant relocation, career changes, or the stress of the Christmas season–it will be hard to create the framework for a relationship to grow. Someone may have spent a lot of time with you during a slowdown in work, but now things are ramping up and there isn't as much time anymore. [That] can be a hint that you have to wait until the dust settles before evaluating whether this can work out.

Timing is not on your side.
You've gone on some fantastic dates, but they're going out of town next month, or they recently acquired a new job that's taking up all of their focus. While the connection is incredible, you can't overlook that other things are occurring in their life that demand their attention, which unavoidably restricts their ability to offer in other areas. King believes if you're finding yourself grieving about some time-related restriction, that's a strong clue it's not the proper moment.

The logistics make it hard to be together.
It may be one of these scenarios: They're in a monogamous relationship with someone else. They have small children, and you aren't sure if you're ready for the burden. You suddenly met them when you were traveling, and you don't sure whether you desire a long-distance relationship. They're hurting from a painful breakup and could be on the rebound. You're smitten with your

boss, but your firm expressly bans romantic interactions at work. Although love is a leap of faith, sometimes the danger is too high to take, and the hurdles are too overwhelming to get through.

One of you is emotionally unavailable.
When you're starting into a relationship with someone, there's an element of extreme vulnerability and honesty required to take your sentiments to the next level and build a genuine passionate connection. If one of you can't engage in that conversation with your complete self (i.e., you're emotionally unavailable), King believes it's a clue that the relationship won't be able to proceed ahead because there are parts of you that will be emotionally inaccessible, which makes it impossible to genuinely know each other.

One of you is just not ready for a relationship.

One of you is healing. Whether it be from bodily, emotional, or spiritual harm, recovery is a time to focus on oneself. While it's not difficult to maintain a strong and loving relationship while mending, this again is a time of change and development that may impact both persons as the recovery progresses.

One of you is not ready to perform the effort required to develop.
When you're in a relationship with someone, the connection might push you beyond your comfort zone as unhealed scars and undiscovered elements of yourself surface. If one of you feels uncomfortable addressing those challenges and can't compromise on your way of life to include someone else, you're not in the appropriate position to

commit to what's fundamental for the relationship to develop.

Your instinct is telling you it's not right.
They're great for you, but you keep feeling that there's something weird about the relationship or something is missing. Although you can't exactly put a finger on it, don't disregard those suspicions. Sometimes even if someone positively hits all of your buttons, it just doesn't seem right. It doesn't have to make sense. Call it a gut feeling or intuition, maybe this is a warning that it's not the proper moment.

What to do next.
If you've concluded you've met someone right at the wrong moment, you can feel sad that you can't get beyond these problems to make the relationship work, but there is something you can do about it. Here are some tips to start processing these

sentiments so you can go on or perhaps make it work down the line:

Pause and reinterpret things from a point of plenty.
It's crucial to approach dating and relationships from a safe position. Instead of seeing things as the right person at the wrong moment, consider adjusting that viewpoint to the right person at the wrong time. There are about eight billion people on Earth. There are so many individuals who you may have a lovely relationship with.

Life is long, and people change. Just because it's not working out with someone right now, it doesn't imply that you've missed out on your one opportunity at happiness.

Life will move on, and there are plenty of possibilities to date [and] maybe even date this perfect person when the time is right. Even if one chance goes, there will be another.

Reflect and investigate the link attentively. This might be one of the toughest things when you're confident you've met the perfect person at the wrong moment. Instead of fixating on them as the solution for your happiness, he advocates asking yourself alternative questions that might self-actualize you toward personal improvement.

Take time to focus on what you need today and where you're heading in life. Yes, this person feels like the right person, but do you need the 'right person? Maybe you need more time to recover. Maybe you need to concentrate on taking care of your body, heart, and soul. Maybe you need to connect more with friends and family. Maybe you need to follow your career where it's going or remain in place. What do you need today and how would this appropriate individual fit, if able?

Consider your attachment style.

"appropriate person" for you is a form of restricting thinking that might show an anxious attachment style, which is distinguished by a fear of being underappreciated—or an avoidant attachment style, where one perceives love from a point of scarcity.

Moving to approach relationships from a more secure position may be fully rid of the concept of the right person, the wrong moment. Dating with a stable attachment style is about seeking a full mate who is ready for you and can satisfy your requirements.

Allow for the actual present, and accept what transpired.

Sometimes closed doors put you back on the road you're designed for. Nguyen suggests letting yourself accept the situation that you're at in life today by enjoying all the good things you do have. "If this individual isn't able to contribute constructively, that's OK. There will be other possibilities for connection, but what's most important is that you're doing what you need for yourself and your priorities. Otherwise, you face the danger of straining yourself to be what someone else needs without caring for yourself."

Cherish them and observe them with appreciation.
it's crucial to appreciate the sensations and lessons this individual helped you experience. Instead of seeing things from regret, strive to love them and respect the lessons they offered you. "Maybe this individual led you to take a serious look at where you're heading in life. That is valuable! The procedure may have been difficult and perhaps extremely essential,"

It's gut-wrenching that you couldn't have them in your life in the manner that you had wanted. But your favorable sentiments for them might continue by viewing them as an occasion for positive development in your life instead of a wasted chance. Sometimes, some individuals are just supposed to be in your life for a brief time to show you that there are a lot of people that can match with you or remind you of the type of life-affirming beauty that love may provide. Plus, it'll make it that much more significant when you do find the ideal person when everything aligns.

How to recognize when it's right.
When it's the right connection, it won't merely be dependent on sheer chance. You'll be at comparable stages in your journey and have a strong, natural desire to do whatever it takes to be in each other's lives. Another indication is that you'll experience minimal tension around them. King says to watch out

for signals that show emotional safety meaning you aren't feeling unsure, provoked, hesitant, or that you have to estimate their next action.

When you're with the right person at the appropriate moment

You're both emotionally accessible and ready for a commitment.
You communicate successfully, honestly, and together.
You don't play games, and neither do they—their actions and enthusiasm match their words.
You feel like you can be yourself, and you don't have to conceal anything.
You may readily discuss topics with them, and they respond honestly, too.
You love spending time together, and it seems secure to be with them.
You can picture yourself establishing a future with them, and they're on the same page.

Your ideas are complementary, and you're both moving in the same direction.
You're able to navigate through disagreement healthily.
You want the best for one other, and there's a lot of respect in the relationship.
You promote their growth as a person and vice versa.
The relationship is demanding in a great manner; you want to bring out the best in each other.
There's a strong connection to each other on all levels—spiritual, intellectual, mental, emotional, and physical.
There's a huge concern for each other's aims and an understanding that seems natural.
If you have a history of being in toxic relationships, and this one seems different, you could be on to something.
Compromise comes easy for the most part; it's something you want to do to sustain the connection instead of feeling like you have to do it.
The bottom line.

Meeting the right person at the wrong moment is the expression of desire in its greatest form. It's exhilarating, but genuine love demands two individuals who feel the relationship is worth working on together. It involves a desire to perform the acts required to build the relationship and have it unfurl wherever it's intended to go.

"If someone is not ready or able to love you in the manner that you deserve to be loved, it is OK to go away and believe that you will find the love you seek and deserve," King adds. "Don't restrict yourself to the right person, wrong moment connection. There's always more love to be discovered that can meet you precisely where you are."

Chapter 2

UNIQUE WAYS TO FALL IN LOVE

How to Fall in Love—Even in the Age of Ghosting and Orbiting

if you're continuously repeating to yourself "I want to fall in love," you first need to be receptive to accepting it.
And, lemme tell you, it isn't so simple. In fact, at times—especially in the era of ghosting, orbiting, cloaking, etc., etc., etc., it might seem plain impossible. So for the benefit of my lonely soul (and the others out there who are also Googling "I want to fall in love" 3 to 15 times a week), I consulted with two relationship gurus about how to fall in love—and, most crucially, how to open your cold, cynical heart to let it happen.

If you can't stop repeating "I want to fall in love: Be conscious of your mindset

My friends and I frequently joke about "putting off a vibe" when it comes to attracting people, and according to the professionals, that's very much a thing. "You've to be receptive to the experience. " If the concept of going out on a date—even a coffee date—is torture, and you discover that you're attempting to placate your friends or family who believe it's time for you to date, you're not open. Maybe you know you're not ready, and you've got to recognize that." The first step to take here is to find out where you are mentally and emotionally so that you can ultimately get to where you want to be in the process.

Change up your strategies for courting a partner

Anyone would be reluctant to date if they continued doing the same activities that did not provide them pleasant outcomes. If things simply keep not working out, probably, part of you will also want to throw up the towel on dating.

But it's not enough to merely declare, 'I despise internet dating.' If you know that about yourself, rather than being reluctant and not open to dating (since you want to meet anyone, you're simply discouraged), seek out different alternatives to the process.

Look for someone for the correct reasons

We've all heard the statement that you can't love someone else if you don't love yourself first. Cliché? For sure. But it's also accurate in certain respects. "I do think we can experience a real falling in love when we perceive that the person complements us perfectly, and not because we look for them to replace an empty part of ourselves that hurts," says psychologist Jorge Fernandez. "When we do the latter, we are seeking a Band-Aid, when what we actually should be looking for is how to permanently fill that hole ourselves. [Then], we are ready to be in love." No one else can make you happy with yourself.

Stop placing so much strain on the situation It may have the opposite effect. "There's an old cliché: Love comes when you least expect it. And I think that's true to some degree," adds Fernandez. "I feel that looking too much drives us to overextend and strive to discover compatibility in individuals who aren't good for it. Be open to the notion that you may discover love, but conduct your life such that it's a wonderful surprise when you find it."

Sure, put yourself out there, but don't go into every drinks date with the assumption that the individual will be "the one." They may simply be "the one" to have a glass of rosé and some truffle fries with, and that's alright, too.

Be alright with the truth that could not work out

Falling in love is terrifying as hell—especially in an age where you may date someone for, like, a long time and then be ghosted out of nowhere. But the anxieties and "what ifs" shouldn't discourage you from being receptive to it. Accept that you may be injured, and that life will carry on if you do, We feel, more than ever, mainly thanks to social media, that love is an easy and uncomplicated thing. It is not. There are several places in which we need to get compatible. We may have passion, physical attraction, and love for the same cuisine and music, yet it still does not ensure a happy relationship. If you want to be open to falling in love, the most crucial step you can take is to understand that your heart may be crushed

Take a break if you need it

If you're straight-up simply not into dating right now, that's okay—give yourself a break. Not everyone should be dating all the time." It's not like, 'Oh you best get on it, it's a goal you have to attain.' If you want a time out, if you need a dating detox, take it. But make sure you're aware of why you're doing it...and then relaunch with a new recipe."

That way, when you do go back out there, you're both intellectually and emotionally equipped to be receptive to the process.

Let's assume your daily wish of "I want to fall in love" appears to have been answered. Here's how you know whether it's love or desire. Plus, what it means to have chemistry with some, according to science.

Chapter 3

WHAT YOU NEED TO KNOW ABOUT LOVE

It is possible to love someone who doesn't love you back. It's not a complete love, it doesn't have a whole lot of depth, but it's still there.

People constantly claim that you have to love yourself before anybody else can love you but that's not actually true. You can be loved even if you detest yourself. It's simply not going to be healthy. It's not going to be the greatest type of love.

Falling in love is nature's drug and you may OD on it.

Emotionally OD. Not, like, genuine death. Ew.

It's so awful to have loved someone once and then never again. Sometimes you'll wish it never occurred just so you didn't know how fantastic it felt.

Then you recall the statement "It's better to have loved and lost than to have ever loved at all" and you're like, "Okay, fine."

You will never love someone exactly the same way you do the first time.

In most circumstances, this is a positive thing. The first time is absolutely wild.

It's a great moment when you discover you are someone who's worth loving.

And it's an even worse time when you briefly forget it.

Sex doesn't always bring people closer. Sometimes it only reveals the faults in the relationship.

That being said, a relationship may survive on excellent sex for a scary period of time.

Someone you love will betray you. You can't get through this life without it.

You can't force yourself to love someone. If it's not there, it's not going to happen. Ever.

Everyone is an idiot when it comes to issues of the heart. Love is the great equalizer. Whenever you feel frightened by someone's coolness, simply imagine them crying in their bedroom after someone destroyed their heart. I promise it's occurred.

Love doesn't always feel like brain orgasms. Sometimes it feels the finest when it's at its most subtle, as when it's 3 p.m. on a Sunday and you're reading a book with your feet intertwined with someone else's on the sofa. You glance about yourself for a second and realize that you've never felt safer.

Ironically, it's the calmer times that will leave the most permanent impact.

Everyone wants to be adored. Everyone wants to depend on someone. For a lot of folks, it's their Achilles heel. Love is the reason why they made most of their blunders.

At its finest, love may feel better than heroin. At its worst, it might feel like heroin withdrawal.

I've never done heroin however so this is entirely supposition.

Finding love is the unconscious motive for a lot of the things we do. It's why we work out, it's why we go to a pub on a Saturday night when we really don't want to, it's why we agree to meet strangers off the internet.

Don't feel ashamed if you've never been in love before. You have a ton of company.

When you fall in love with someone, be prepared for the chance that you could despise them one day.

You will always have that one ex who will stay in your memory. They'll feel like a continual dull pain in your side.

Love will transform you become the finest and worst version of yourself, often in the same night.

Love is the reason why we're all here. Well, most of us anyhow.

Trace the wounds life has given you. It will remind you that at one time, you battled for something. You believed.
Trace the wounds life has given you. It will remind you that at one time, you battled for something. You believed.
"You are the only one who gets to determine whether you are happy or not—do not put

your happiness into the hands of other people. Do not make it reliant on their approval of you or their affection for you. At the end of the day, it doesn't matter whether someone hates you or if someone doesn't want to be with you. All that counts is that you are content with the person you are becoming. All that counts is that you enjoy yourself and that you are proud of what you are sending out into the world. You are in command of your delight, of your value. You get to be your own validation. Please don't ever forget that.

Chapter 4

THINGS TO REMEMBER WHEN YOU'RE FALLING IN LOVE

Love may be scary... and you're entitled to be experiencing a lot of strong emotions.

“I'm really beginning to fall for someone... and it's been a while since I've been in a relationship. Is there anything I should be looking out for? Common pitfalls that individuals slip into, etc.?”

There's nothing like the exciting surge of new love. Your brain is being inundated with big amounts of happy hormones and it might seem like you're high around the clock.

What are they doing? Are they thinking about me right now? Whatever they're doing, I hope they're happy. What would we fight about in the long term? Am I already becoming too clingy? How do our names sound together? Should I not have texted them that item yesterday? Where would our perfect holiday be? Do they enjoy the same activities as me?

Our imaginations go amok conducting mental acrobatics over our new love interest.

To help you keep your feet (slightly) planted during this new and exciting time, here are things to remember while you're falling in love with someone new.

You're entitled to feel thrilled

Yes, you are going to be distracted as thoughts of them fly through your mind... and that's absolutely OK.

Going into a new relationship is an exciting transitional moment. You're allowed to feel happy/giddy/distracted/joyful about it.

Instead of opposing it or attempting to understand it, accept it. Let the thrill take its course through your body. Every feeling you encounter is there for a purpose, and this surge of exhilaration is likely there to educate you that "This one counts. You care about this one. So lean into it."

You're permitted to experience some anxiety Along with the surge of excitement that comes with a new love interest, you're also likely to experience some mix of nervousness and/or worry.

Opening up to a new relationship may cause a lot of dread, anxiety, and worry in individuals. Maybe you fear that they're too wonderful to be true, or that they won't like you back. Love is a risk...it always is.

And just like the exhilaration we just touched on, you're also permitted to enjoy the worry. You might welcome it into your body and tell it "You have a home here. Thank you for watching out for me." That's not to mean that you'll necessarily want to let that feeling dominate your head and all of your thoughts... nevertheless there's no purpose in denying its presence in your body.

Don't let your life go to the wayside

Some individuals have a propensity to forsake their friends, family, duties, and hobbies when they start dating someone new. I understand how enticing this pattern is (after all, you want to see them/touch them/taste them all the time!) but it isn't helping you or strengthening your young relationship's foundation.

It's crucial to maintain doing the things that make you happy that aren't related to your new significant other. If 100% of your emotional satisfaction comes from your new partner, you may ultimately start to resent them for taking up so much of your time and they could begin to feel restricted by you, knowing well well that they give the bulk of your pleasure. We all need numerous avenues to pleasure and fulfillment... and although there's nothing wrong with being with a partner who you feel delighted to be with, you should also experience joy from other sources in your life.

If this moment is especially challenging for you, proactively reach out to one or two of your closest friends and directly tell them "Hey, I'm beginning to fall for this person and I want to make sure that I maintain being myself and I don't get fully sucked into it... and I also cherish our friendship and want to continue to engage in it. Can you help hold me accountable to hanging out with you every week or two, just to make sure that I'm not simply spending time with (your new love interest's name)? That would assist me out a lot."

Keep doing the things that make you you, and keep seeing the people who you feel light up by (in your relationship with your significant other and outside of it)... and your relationship will thank you.

Chapter 5

LEAVING THE BEST THINGS BEHIND

When To Leave Things Behind

I have left certain things behind. And even though I know where to locate them. I also realize that life is sometimes a one-way path. But I'm not frightened of or regret anything since I know what's worth fighting for and which conflicts are meaningless.

How many things have you given up on and left behind in your life? Sometimes it's hard to grasp that with every effort we put into them, everything and everyone we leave behind is like smoke leaving through an open window.

This might be hard for us to accept because of the emotional energy we invest into the people and events of our life. Until disappointment strikes, until that moment occurs in which we discover that the scale of life is a little off balance. That we're left with nothing to offer and have gotten nothing in return. And that the dream was a nightmare.

Have we done anything wrong? Should we maybe regret all of our actions? Never. He who doesn't battle for his dream isn't courageous. He who doesn't battle for his aspirations and fantasies will never reach the moon. Feel proud of that fortitude, but remember that sometimes giving up is the smartest and most logical thing to do.

Some conflicts are useless...
a woman clutching a realistic heart
Let's start by establishing a crucial point straight: No one realizes that a war or a dream has been fruitless until reality, in all its agony, slaps them in the face.

It doesn't matter whether we're talking about a career, a friendship, or a romance. Life is a continuous sequence of moments that put us to the test, of chapters we should appreciate, strive for and learn from. Because learning is the fundamental key that maintains our life.

It's probable that you've made some blunders and that at this point, you've given up on and left behind numerous things. Should you regret them? Not at all. To lament a mistake is to fuel resentment and lose out on a learning chance.

Mistakes must be recognized, comprehended, processed, and incorporated into what we call our "storage of experience." And if such encounters bring us terrible memories, don't feed or pursue these sentiments. Unpleasant memories should be swapped for the here and now, for today's enjoyment.

No conflict is wasted since it is a life lived and experience garnered. Nonetheless, if something isn't serving you, it's crucial to know when to leave it behind. We must realize when a person or activity doesn't worth what we're giving up or suffering for it.

When should we leave anything behind?
sketching girl and paper boats
It may seem like an obvious question, but it's not. That's why we're going to dig deeper into it. At this second a lot of us may be fostering dreams and projects that don't worth our time and energy.

Let's evaluate this:

The power of mistaken expectations
Sometimes we make the mistake of blaming others for feeding our false hopes, while in truth that duty belongs on our shoulders. Some individuals put their sights on that

ideal job when it's probable they're not even equipped or qualified for it.

There are always individuals who put all of their emotions and anxiety on a person who truly has never even given them an indication that they feel anything for them. It's OK to dream but we must constantly keep objectivity, balance, and perspective.

Emotional cost

Emotions are truly a very strong and hazardous engine. Sometimes they make us offer our everything, till our very last breath for that significant other, for that beloved desire.

birds connected to the moon

We don't perceive the limitations and we open our hearts without reading the instruction manual. That handbook should instruct us right from the beginning to "be cautious, watch out for yourself, safeguard your self-esteem." Nevertheless, we don't always do it.

We should learn to be more receptive, to persuade ourselves that we too deserve to receive. Does that friendship provide you support, complicity, respect, and acknowledgment? Then go ahead.

Does that partnership provide you happiness? Does it nourish your hopes? Does it invest in you as much as you do in them? Does the other person give up things for you as you've had to do for them on occasion? If not, evaluate this and make a choice.

We should give up and leave behind anything or anybody that feeds on selfishness. That doesn't recognize us and pulls from our power and dreams instead of enhancing us. Move forward and lock doors and leave them behind. You know very well where they are, but you also know where you want to go.

Chapter 6

LOVING SOMEONE YOU CANNOT HOLD UNTO

"Attraction may come at any moment even if it is towards someone you cannot have. Try to confirm that it is not your fault while also emphasizing the importance of your life without being with them.

We don't get to pick who or what we are attracted to. Whether from how we were reared, what we've learned, experiences in former relationships, or simply genetics, the sensation of excitement we receive from things and people is mostly out of our control. Most of the time, this is a good experience. The exhilaration of a new relationship and the constant pleasure of excelling in a pastime don't question when something makes us feel good. We shape our lives around attaining more of the things we desire.

However, there are occasions when what we desire is something we cannot have. Sometimes it's because of money, sometimes we don't live in the right area at the appropriate time, and sometimes it's because we are simply attracted to someone even though we know it won't work out. Even if you are sincerely and deeply in love with someone else, it doesn't imply you can pursue it.

When we are unable of following through on a connection that we really want, it may be terrible. It might make you doubt your sanity, question your life, and leave you feeling empty and miserable. The rest of the world gets to be with anyone they want, but not you. It feels unjust. It is unjust. But sentiments aren't fair; they are.

Loving someone, you can't have is tough. However, it can be overcome. It may seem ridiculous to want to try to go out of love with someone, but there are times it is required. It will need patience and self-compassion. In this post, you will discover what to do if you love someone you can't have and how to let go.

Why Should You Work To Get Out Of Love?

Human beings are attracted to seeking connection. We have biological impulses that promote and reward us for creating meaningful connections. Companionship, sex, love, creating a family, all of these things, and more are significant motivators. If you have these sentiments for other people and think you have the strength and ability to act on those impulses, it's rewarding when you do.

This is why it may be so hurtful and challenging when you feel powerless to act on your love for someone else. That suffering is unlikely to dissipate or reduce unless you make an attempt to modify your life in some manner. Our sensations of desire are highly convoluted. However, by altering our circumstances, we may modify the conditions of our sentiments, which can diminish them.

How Does An Unachievable Attachment Develop?

Almost everyone has, at some time in their lives, felt pulled to someone they couldn't be with. Whether it was a high school infatuation for someone you never talked to or being pulled to a married colleague, it may happen anywhere at any moment. However, even though these sentiments might come up without surprise, numerous factors make you more likely to develop unattainable love.

Breakups are traumatic. It may almost be like losing part of your mind, depending on how long you were together. When you move from having your romantic reward circuits activated practically daily to having just yourself for companionship, it's understandable to want to find anything and anybody to feel better. People who have recently separated are more prone to acquire reckless sentiments of attachment in general, even when it's hard to act on.

A History of Codependency: Being codependent contains a big component of wanting other people to justify your existence and worth. Without other people telling you that you matter, you spiral out into negative thinking. When it feels like your only alternatives are finding anybody you can to love you or being brutally alone, you are more inclined to attempt to find love with someone you can't be with.

Grappling with Depression: Similar to the previous two, persons suffering from depression are in a dark place that they feel unable to alter. Whether transitory or permanent, anybody who comes along and alleviates the depression may be a huge comfort, even for a short time. Just like how sadness raises your chance of addictive behaviors, depression makes you more prone to desiring love you can't have.

Strong Non-Romantic Relationships: You have an attractive colleague with whom you click. You have a close female buddy who gets all your jokes and likes the same activities. Romance may pop up when you least expect it. Once it happens, it's hard to shut off. If you have one or more persons in your life with whom you have, even passionate, attachments through common hobbies, there's an enhanced likelihood for romantic attachment to emerge, even if it's purely one-sided.

What Can Make Love Unattainable?

Several basic impediments might stand in the way of you and another individual ever having a connection.

You Have Feelings For An Ex: It's fairly rare, when a relationship ends, for one of the parties to still experience sentiments of fondness, even intense ones. If breakups leave us aching for some connection, you might easily pull towards someone you've previously experienced that connection with. However, odds are things ended for a cause, and if they've moved on and you haven't, you love someone you can't have.

They Don't Feel The Same Way:

When romantic sentiments emerge on one side of a non-romantic relationship (e.g., close friends), you might be trapped attempting to generate a sense of chemistry or spark with someone who isn't interested.

Your Lives Are Too Different: You can meet someone at a party that appears like the ideal mate for you. Then you find out they reside on the opposite side of the nation. As fast as you got enthused about someone, they're gone. Unfortunately, your sentiments didn't depart at the same moment.

The Relationship Would Violate Social Norms: Even if you are head-over-heels in love with someone currently in a relationship or married, you can't do anything about it. They've decided to be with someone else. You may believe they should be with you, but that's not your decision to make.

What Do You Do To Let Go?

There are two main circumstances worth examining when it comes to letting go of unachievable love. One, you have lately discovered that you may have emotions for someone and want to start performing the effort of attempting to detach yourself before things grow too serious. Two, you are in love with someone else. You tried breaking away, but the sentiments are still there, and it's getting to be a significant issue. If you've lately recognized you may have affections for someone:

Take some time to assess how much of a presence this individual has in your life. If you needed to back off to safeguard your emotions, what would that take? How much time do you spend thinking about them or attempting to be near them? Is there another way you can spend your time that would be better for you?
Talk to your mutual pals. If you actually have emotions for someone, you've undoubtedly done one thing or another that has signified your desire. Tell them you are beginning to grow worried about where

those sentiments are leading and speak about how you want to move through them. Set appropriate boundaries with the object of your passion. This might be challenging, but it's necessary. Putting up barriers to being near or with your sweetheart might seem irrational. However, your emotions for the other person undoubtedly evolved since you were spending a lot of time together. Setting some restrictions on how frequently or how long you are near each other is a wonderful place to start.

Take some time to assess your connection with the other person generally. What encounters are most stressful or most generate thoughts of love? Are there instances when you feel like you can't control your attraction to them? If you can map out when it seems safe to be near them and when you should stay away, it will make it simpler to start getting over it.

The list above is a broad technique for you to start getting a handle on the nature of your connection with the other person and take proper actions to prevent it from growing. Sometimes such prophylactic work is no longer a possibility. Your sentiments are intense, and you need to break free. Here's what you can do to start extricating yourself.

Be honest with yourself about what you are suffering with. Love is great, and love is horrible. It is alright to confess that you are caught up in a love that is the latter sort. It is, in fact, crucial to the long-term welfare that you realize you are in pain.

Reach out to friends and relatives. They almost surely know that you are suffering from this. Let them know that you need their aid and that you want things to change. Work with them to find out precisely what needs to change and how to achieve it. You will need this support because if you are genuinely in love, you cannot be an impartial judge of how horrible things are.

Start restricting your interaction with the other individual. They may be the best person in the world. Obviously, they are fantastic for you. But they are also a constant cause of considerable anguish. It will take time, but you need to start lowering the quantity of time you spend with one another. Whether you see them less, cease seeing them alone, or limit your time together to shorter, whatever it takes to lessen continuous attraction.

Consider telling the other person how you feel. In the end, your connection with this other person has to change for your protection. This may be attainable via your actions. However, the other person may notice the difference and attempt to reconnect. At that moment, it may be vital to be upfront that, even though you know it can never happen, you have deep emotions for them, and you are pulling back to protect yourself.

One-Sided Love Can Be Miserable

We tend to conceive of love as this fantastic and lovely experience. We wish to discover someone we can be entirely honest with, someone we can depend on for surviving life's challenges and reveling in triumph. However, when that desire and passion are unrequited and can never be achieved, it may make everything else seem wrong. What's the purpose, after all, of everything you accomplish if you can't be with who you want to be with?

This state of mind is something that can be worked through. Chances are, there are underlying motives behind your desire that can be modified. There is definitely a way you interpret the world and yourself, creating this false prison for your ideas and emotions. By practicing self-care and contemplation, utilizing your support networks, and exploring new avenues for satisfaction, you may work your way toward a more centered state of mind. This will also more likely lead to a relationship with someone who will love you back.

Friends, family, and self-improvement may lead you a long way.

You don't have to conquer your sentiments on your own.

Everyone has been lured by something we can't have. For some of us, it means wanting a person we can't be with. If you love someone you can't have, it will only help to take the time to understand why you desire something unreachable and how to go over it. Learning to let go may be liberating.

Chapter 7

TIRED OF EVERYTHING

The world that we live in is a stressful place to be. It is worn. It is thankless. It is continuously hard and barely gratifying. You're exhausted simply because you live in it. You're weary of loving too much, caring too much, giving too much to a world that never offers anything back. You are weary of investing in indeterminate results. You're weary of uncertainty. Tired of grey.

I know you haven't always been this worn out - that there was a time when you were optimistic and pure. When your optimism surpassed your skepticism and you had a limitless amount in you to share. I know you have been chipped at and worn down piece by piece — a broken heart here and an un-kept promise there. I know the world hasn't always been kind during the games you've played and that you've lost more times than you have ever won. I know you're feeling unmotivated to try again. I know.

Because the reality is, we're all exhausted. Every single one of us. By a certain age, we are all nothing more than an army of broken hearts and suffering souls, hopelessly yearning for fulfillment. We want more yet we're too exhausted to ask for it. We're sick of where we are yet we are too terrified to begin afresh. We need to take chances yet we're frightened to see it all come tumbling down around us. After all, we're not sure how many times we will be allowed to start anew.

We all assume we're alone in our tiredness. But the fact is we're weary of each other - tired of the games we play and the falsehoods we tell and the uncertainty we portray to one other. We don't want to play the villain but we don't want to play the idiot either. So our guards go up. Our defenses rile. And we take on the part that we despise to see portrayed because we're not sure what option we have left.

I know how tough it might seem to continue striving and giving and being when you are drained right through to the soul. I realize that the cheery ideas you were once offered now feel worn and dismal. But here's what I ask if you're this close to giving up: give it one more go, with emotion. I know you're bored with your efforts. I realize that you're at your wit's end. But the reality about that second wind of passion is that you're never going to recognize you have it if you do not carry on sprinting through your first.

We're all more resilient than we realize, and that's an obvious reality. There is always more love that we are capable of giving, more optimism that we are capable of feeling, and more passion that we're capable of releasing and pouring out into the world. We simply don't travel far enough down our own pathways to reach the point where we're seeing those acts pay off. We desire quick results and when we see none, we give up. We let the tiredness stop us. We feel angry with the lack of input and we believe that means we have to chuck the whole endeavor straight out the window.

Because here's something we all dread to confess - none of us are inspired every day. We all become fatigued. We all get disheartened. And we're permitted to work on through those emotions. Just because you're beaten down and worn out and sick of the life that you're living doesn't mean you're not making a change. Every individual you have ever respected has experienced periods when they felt absolutely defeated in the pursuit of their ambitions. But it didn't prevent them from reaching them. You're permitted to stumble slowly toward your largest changes. It doesn't necessarily have to be a flaming, brazen affair.

Some elements of life happen silently. They happen slowly. They happen because of the modest, meticulous decisions that we make daily, which evolve us into better versions of ourselves. We have to give ourselves the time to let such modifications happen. To see them develop. To not get hopelessly disillusioned in the in-between.

When you're fatigued, go gently. Go softly. Go timidly. But do not stop. You are exhausted for all the right reasons. You are weary because you're meant to be. You're exhausted because you're making a change. You are fatigued for all the right reasons and it's merely an indicator to carry on. You are fatigued because you're expanding. And eventually, that growth will give way to the precise rejuvenation that you need.

Chapter 8

STOP WAITING FOR THEM TO COME BACK

They are not coming back. And the sooner you accept this, the faster you will be able to collect the shattered parts of your heart and go on.

I know there's a part of you that desires they grasp what they lost, or that they reach out to you to make apologies or sorry, or that they just realize they should've valued you when you were in their life.

But your healing shouldn't be reliant on that, your value shouldn't be contingent on how much they believe they lost out once you left.

Until you don't understand that they aren't coming back, you won't fully be able to go on. Repeat after me - they are not coming back, and I need to learn to live without them. They aren't. They won't. And if, by the rules of nature that conform to a design far greater than ourselves, they do - you should not be sitting there waiting for them.

You must realize that some individuals go because they're supposed to, sometimes things don't go as you intended and, more often than not, you must travel on a route that you didn't want to because it is what is best for you. The journey is bordered with sadness and filled with tears, with the brutal truth of life as an open field in front of you and a bucketload of memories left on the vast road behind.

And that is alright since they were a lesson for you - the finest lesson that you could have gotten.

The lesson that teaches you not to glue your happiness to a single person, especially someone who didn't know where to place you in their life, a lesson that teaches you that people are imperfect and prone to making mistakes and that you must stop searching for dreams in them and start forming dreams of your own.

Dreams that solely rely on you to fulfill them.

And it is generally the most arduous experiences that gift us with incredible strength and the potential to become the finest versions of ourselves.

It is a lesson that teaches you about love – that love is not one-sided or hesitant about you, love is not one foot in and one foot out, and love does not lead you on just to abandon you or let you go.

And I hope you take them as a lesson that teaches you to stop counting the reasons why they should be loved and start listing the numerous reasons why you are the one who is worth loving.

Stop waiting around. It's like gambling with your life. That concern that they'll suddenly erupt into a better person in a better relationship with someone else is misplaced because just like fear indicates it's not happening, waiting around means it (the relationship) isn't happening either.

Remember, while you're waiting around, it indicates you're unavailable for an available relationship.

Chapter 9

LETTING GO

We've all had an ex that we can't seem to get out of our heads. A toxic relationship we hang on to even if it exhausts us. Or even a family member who is harmful. Why can't we learn how to let go of someone, even when we know they're not healthy for us? Holding on is a normal human impulse – yet it's also a fundamental method that we block ourselves from accomplishing our objectives. Because ultimately, not knowing how to move on effects you: It keeps you from attaining your entire potential.

Why is letting go so hard?
Why do we have so many problems learning how to let go of someone we love? We tend to cling to things, events, and particularly people because it meets our desire for certainty. Certainty is one of the six human

needs that influence every choice we make. Letting go and moving on from a relationship frequently implies a huge degree of uncertainty. Even if your relationship had reached its end or one or both of you were unhappy, there was still a level of predictability there that was comfortable.

Sometimes we use the past to justify our present actions, and that's why we can't figure out how to let go. Remember when you were rejected by multiple possible partners in high school or college? Those occasions might make your stay in a relationship – even one that is not good for you – because you are frightened you won't find anybody else. Those memories justify everything for you. When you're unwilling to let go, those memories become a part of your "story" and work against you.

Signs you haven't move on

Learning how to let go of someone you love – someone you've formed a strong connection with and whom you've spent your life with – is likely one of the toughest things you'll ever have to do. That's why so many individuals split up, yet never actually find how to go on. If these indicators seem familiar, you may be one of those people:

You're constantly thinking about what may have been
You think about the individual frequently, or at a time when you'd prefer not
You spend a lot of time remembering memories or searching for them on social media
You bring them up regularly while chatting with friends
When you're feeling bad, they're the first person you think to call
You make adjustments to your life or look to get them back
You feel nervous or even furious when you encounter the person\sYou blame them or

desire to exact vengeance for perceived slights

Letting go of someone you love isn't easy, but clinging on simply holds you back from the chance of an incredible connection. To concentrate your attention on living positively and proactively, you need to learn how to move on. Are you ready to let go of relationships that no longer benefit you?

How to let go of someone :

Knowing you need to let go and letting go are two very different things. These recommendations can help you learn how to move on once and for all.

Recognize when it's time :

Learning when it's time to let go is typically the hardest aspect of this process. But in many circumstances, it's vital to let go to unlock the life you deserve. Though each relationship is different, most believe it's time to end things when the relationship causes them more grief than pleasure or when trust has deteriorated to the point where the passion cannot be rekindled. Deciding how to let go gets simpler when you are confident the moment has arrived and that your future happiness relies on a fresh start.

Identify limiting beliefs:
Do ideas like “I could never be alone” or “I’ll never find someone else who loves me” continuously pass through your mind? Understand that these are not realities - they are limiting beliefs, and although thoughts cancan create your reality, you have the power to modify them. Replace them with powerful ideas such as, “I am open to what the world has in store for me” and “I love myself and deserve the best.” You may feel ridiculous at first, but as you practice these positive incantations as part of your everyday routine, you will notice improvements.

Change your story :

Your narrative is what you tell yourself to rationalize your actions and is based on your limiting beliefs. For example, you convince yourself you can't have a good relationship because of how you grew up. Your parents fought in front of you all the time and finally split. You can't let go of the assumption that all relationships are going to fail, and this is why you can't sustain a good love connection. You use your previous event to explain your present life situation – but you can adjust your tale so that your history supports you instead of holding you down. Your past is not your future unless you live there.

Stop the blame game:

Letting go of someone you love doesn't mean you have to ignore reality, but don't allow it to impact your present course. It is human nature to point the fault at someone else or a prior experience instead of yourself. This is why you blame your significant other after the end of a relationship or another person for anything horrible that occurred to you. Yet even when the facts are dreadful or tragic, you cannot let poor events control your destiny. Instead, use your experiences as a tool to drive you to learn and develop so you can establish a good connection with someone else.

Embrace the "forgive"word:
Going your way does not have to be an event fraught with anger or judgment. When you see that the person is hindering you from developing or reaching your ambitions, you may forgive them and also forgive yourself for whatever sorrow the separation may bring and wish them the best for the future. Remind yourself that to make room for a new, healthy relationship, you must learn how to let go of the old one. Practicing forgiveness is an opportunity to develop and live in the uncertainty of what's ahead.

Master your emotions:

When a relationship ends, it's typical to experience great levels of rage and resentment – particularly if you were not the one who chose to stop it. Maybe at first, you felt virtuous about it, like the anger was helping you go ahead. However, after some time has gone, you start to understand that it's unhealthy for you, and you're not sure how to let go of someone you love and move on with your life.

Negative sentiments take a toll on your mental and physical health – anger is even related to heart disease – and will influence your future relationships. Recognizing this habit as harmful is the first step in the process of letting go. If you're seeking an answer on how to go on, you are already on the proper route. The good news is that in the process of learning how to let go, you may also learn how to manage your emotions.

Practice empathy:
Learning how to move on from a relationship that previously gave you pleasure may be quite tough. When you're letting go of someone, it's useful to think about all sides of the narrative and understand the issue from their point of view. Look at this individual from the same position of compassion and empathy as you did when you were happy together. Yes, your ex may have damaged you, but they likely did not do it out of malice. They believed their needs weren't being satisfied in your relationship and they chose to take action to enhance their emotional condition.

letting go of someone you love

Adopt an attitude of gratitude:
As Tony says, "When you are appreciative, fear leaves and plenty appears." That's why cultivating appreciation is the cure to the pain and worry you experience when you're

learning how to let go of someone. Let go of your expectations and concentrate on appreciation for what you previously shared. This tiny alteration in your viewpoint will help you recognize that life occurs for you, not to you. When you're able to identify the lesson in every event and be thankful for it, you'll lessen the resentment you feel against the other person and instead enjoy what you acquired from the connection.

Talk to someone you trust:
Holding your emotions within simply keeps you locked and may ultimately evolve into anxiety or even grow into depression. Talk to a sympathetic friend, a family member, or a therapist about how you feel, and allow them to be there for you in your time of need. Talking to someone you trust may also help you identify an unhealthy connection and deter you from continuing to go back to that person. Once you commit to learning how to let go of someone, you may even

uncover other times and circumstances you can afford to move on from as well.

Stay off social media:
Learning how to let go of someone you love becomes much more difficult when you are continually reminded of them. Though social media is a method to remain in contact with friends and family, it's the opposite of what you need when you are going through a breakup. Staying off social media while you recover not only avoids you from seeing photographs or postings from your ex, but it will also save you from seeing other happy relationships, which might make you feel worse about your position.

Take care of yourself:
The process of letting go and moving on from a relationship may be hard and lonely. This is not the time to beat yourself up or neglect your needs. When you practice self-care and take this time to fall in love

with yourself, you'll recover more thoroughly and possibly be healthier than you were before the relationship ever began. Indulge in massages or other calming activities, participate in hobbies that make you happy, and concentrate on finding pleasure without being part of a partnership.

Keep busy:
Staying in bed all day and avoiding friends and loved ones makes letting go and moving on that much more difficult. Start your day with an empowering morning ritual that includes activities like priming, meditation, yoga, or writing, then get up and get active. Join clubs, volunteer for a new project at work, or meet a buddy for lunch or drinks. Staying active can help take your mind off the split and enable your wounds to start mending.

Take the time to heal:

Letting go of someone you love is a process. You won't learn how to do it overnight, particularly if you've spent your life clinging on to things you loved – even if, deep down, you knew they weren't appropriate for you. Focusing on moving ahead and building a new narrative for yourself can help you cope with the inevitable sorrow that comes following a breakup. It will also help you avoid blame, build inspiring beliefs to live by, and move on with an open heart.

Even if you know how to let go of someone you love and follow all the procedures, don't expect to feel better instantly. Grieving is natural and you need to give yourself the proper amount of time to experience your feelings. Treat yourself with kindness and don't allow others to shame you into "just getting over it." Though you don't want to isolate yourself, take some extra time away from social events if you feel you need it, and never agree to a date or set-up until you feel you're ready – those who don't give themselves enough time often end up in rebound relationships that are harmful or that prolong the healing process even more.

Learn to let go and move on

Remember that refusing to let go will not bring someone you care about the back. Continuing to hang on simply affects your mental and physical well-being, prohibiting you from completely enjoying life. Embrace life in the present and recognize that uncertainty may be lovely if you look at it from the proper viewpoint.

The key to letting go of someone you love is acknowledging what has occurred, understanding that you can't alter it, and then moving on. Once you're ready to move on and embrace the progress that came from the relationship, greater chances will present themselves. You will have successfully learned how to let go of someone you love and may begin crafting your new tale.

www.ingramcontent.com/pod-product-compliance
Lightning Source LLC
LaVergne TN
LVHW050335160826
845677LV00014B/3622
* 9 7 9 8 3 5 5 3 0 0 3 9 5 *